First Printing, 2018
Wild Cabbage Books
wildcabbagebooks.com

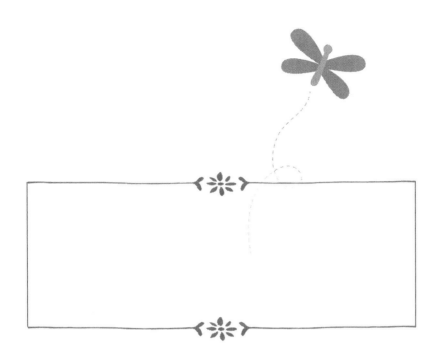

Each of us is limitless; each of us with his
or her right upon the earth.

– Walt Whitman

This above all: to thine ownself be true.

- Shakespeare

Excellence is not an act, but a habit.

– Aristotle

No act of kindness, no matter how small, is
ever wasted.

— Aesop

The way to be happy is to make others so.

– Robert Ingersoll

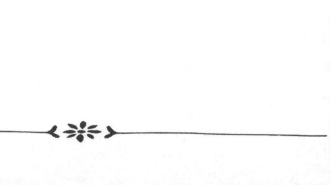

Be happy for this moment. This
moment is your life.

- Omar Kayyam

Peace is always beautiful.

– Walt Whitman

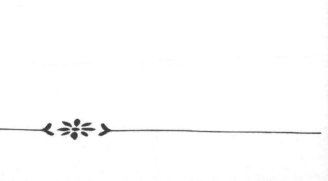

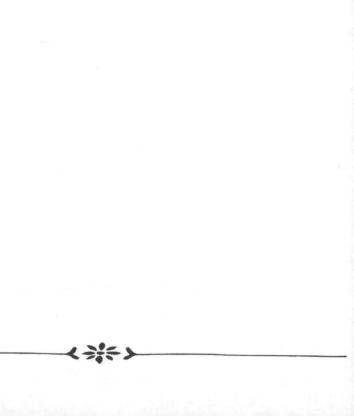

The greatest mistake you can make in life is to be continually fearing you will make one.

– Elbert Hubbard

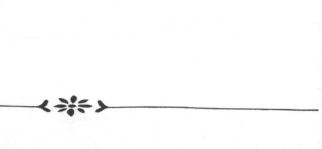

Bloom where you are planted.

- 1 Corinthians KJV

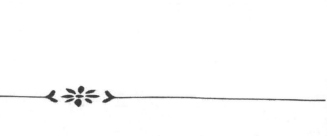

Manufactured by Amazon.ca
Bolton, ON